dogs in their gardens

DOGS
in their | gardens

Page Dickey

STEWART, TABORI & CHANG

New York

Project editor: Sandra Gilbert
Production: Pamela Schechter

Published in 2001 by
STEWART, TABORI & CHANG
A Company of La Martinière Groupe
115 West 18th Street
New York, NY 10011

Library of Congress Cataloging-in-Publication Data
Dickey, Page.
Dogs in their gardens / Page Dickey.
p. cm.
ISBN 1-58479-125-X
1. Dogs—United States. 2. Dogs—Europe.
3. Dogs—United States—Pictorial works. 4. Dogs—Europe—
Pictorial works. 5. Gardens—United States.
6. Gardens—Europe. 7. Gardens—United States—
Pictorial works. 8. Gardens—Europe—Pictorial works. I. Title.

SF426.2.D53 2001
636.7'0887—dc21

2001032827

Title page: Mango, Tim Rees's ruby King Charles spaniel in
his London garden. Bernese mountain dogs, Theodora
and Winston, in their Long Island summer garden.

Copyright page: Truff, my rough-coat Jack Russell terrier,
on thyme in the herb garden.

Dedication page: Our miniature dachsund, Noodle,
in front of a May border.

Table of Contents page: Standard poodles, Scarlet and Aretha,
in the pool garden; black labrador, Buddy, with blue hydrangeas
on Cape Cod; the young spaniel, Springer, poses in front of his
garden on Long Island Sound; bearded collies, Lizzy and
Maggie, with Joe-Pye weed in South Salem, New York; Fauna
and Michael Brennan on their deck in Syracuse.

Introduction page: Jack Russell terrier Chloe surveys
the garden from an apple tree.

Page 96: Barnsley walks the rose allée at Madoo.

The text of this book was composed
in Humanist typeface.

Printed in Singapore

10 9 8 7 6 5 4 3 2 1
First Printing

I want first to thank all the
dog and garden owners in the book for their
enthusiasm and patience—Nola Anderson and
Jim Mullen, Serena Bass, Steve Bell, Sir William
and Lady Benyon, Craig Bergmann and James
Grigsby, Chotsie and Allan Blank, Michael
Brennan, Oonie Burley, Dick Button, Frank and
Anne Cabot, Lucy Close, Tom Connell,
Arabella and Nat Dane, Robert Dash, Sarah
and Scotty Dunbar, Sydney Eddison, Bill and
Nancy Frederick, Carol Goldberg, Dennis
Grimaldi, Jai Imbrey, Jackie and Peter
Kamenstein, Nancy McCabe, Ngaere Macray
and David Seeler, Kitty May, Pepe and John
Maynard, Jennifer Myers, Richard Oldfield and
Amicia de Moubray, Melissa Orme, Irina
Ourusoff, Jean and Don Quaintance, Tim Rees,
Renny Reynolds and Jack Staub, John Rosselli,
David and Susan Rubin, Barbara Shattuck,
Gabrielle and Alex Sheshunoff, Sir Reresby and
Lady Sitwell, Katie Spitz and Dan Rhodes, Susy
and Coleman Townsend, Kathie Weymouth,
Bunny Williams, Nina Wood, Devon and Eli
Zabar, and Robin Zitter.

My thanks go also to my agent Janis Donnaud,
and to Leslie Stoker, my publisher and fellow dog
lover. I am endlessly grateful to Sandy Gilbert,
Emily Von Kohorn, Jennie McGregor Bernard,
and Alexandra Maldonado who, with hard work
and unflagging humor, made my collection of
doggy words and pictures into a finished book.
And, finally, I thank my husband, Bosco Schell,
for his daily encouragement and support.

For Jean, Scott, Kim, and Keith who
grew up with dogs in their gardens

table of contents

introduction

How dull a garden seems to me without a dog disrupting its calmness, breaking the hard-edged symmetry by lying across its paths, rolling on the panels of lawn, enjoying the aspect at the top of a knoll, sniffing the air, nosing the flowers. Gardening is at best a solitary pursuit–planting, weeding, pruning, deadheading, stepping back to appraise the results–a time to lose oneself musing, daydreaming. And yet, most of us want some sort of companionship that will give comfort but not disturb our thoughts. What is more ideal than one or two dogs lying close by, silently following our activities?

Of course, canines periodically play havoc in gardens, lifting hind legs on the boxwood to mark their prized territory or digging holes in the perennial border after the elusive vole. Our puppies, Noodle and Roux, not yet understanding the elegance of walking on paths, pad across our garden beds, tumbling among the tender seedlings. The plastic Haws watering can that stands by the spigot has a handle deeply notched with the tooth marks of May, my old Scottish deerhound, reminding me poignantly of the days when she was young. My indispensable rubber kneeling pad looks like a piece of Swiss cheese.

But dogs who reside in well-loved gardens soon learn to respect the rules of their flow-ery domain. They ornament their surroundings and become identified with them. "Dogs are the soft underbelly of every gardener," says English landscape designer, Tim Rees. In fact, gardeners are often as crazy about their dogs as they are about their flowers.

This relationship of dog, man, and garden is hardly new. Vita Sackville-West was rarely seen strolling along her borders without her Alsatian by her side. Edith Wharton's parterres were peopled with her Pekingese. Lawrence Johnston's adored dachshunds were at his feet or tucked under his arm as he strolled through his garden rooms at Hidcote. In the following pages, you will meet an astonishing assortment of dogs gracing some favorite gardens of today.

two-garden
SCOTTIES

Roxie and Fife, ink-black Scottish terriers who disprove the breed's reputation for dourness, frolic in their Wilmington, Delaware garden all winter and spring. But for the summer, they move with their devoted owners, Susy and Coleman Townsend, to their other digs—a cool, crisp, sparkling garden on a mountainside in New Hampshire.

Coleman, a passionate gardener, planned the southern garden for winter and spring interest, using formal, geometric lines near the house. He built a stone terrace and paths and planted trees in rows, underplanting with ground covers and bulbs. The result is eye-pleasing structure, spring color, and easy maintenance. A small square pool on the terrace offers the sound of water as well as fascination for two curious Scotties. Sometimes it distracts

▲ Fife and Roxie, merely appearing at odds in their Delaware spring garden. Fife surveys the dogwood-laced woods from the square pool on the terrace where water spills into a smaller pool below.

them from the deliciously muddy ground at the far corner of the property where a stream overflows.

Black dogs (especially Scottish sorts) wilt in the muggy summer heat south of New York. So, for that matter, do most perennials, let alone gardeners. But in northern New England, both flourish during diamond days and sweater nights. Five-year-old Roxie and two-year-old Fife tear up and down their New Hampshire hillside (that is, as far as the invisible fence allows them to go) in pursuit of woodchucks. Or, they chase each other in front of the bold border of yellow and silver-leaved perennials Coleman tends with the help of garden designer Bill Noble. Just occasionally they will pause in profile, thinking serious thoughts, their sturdy, square outlines at once dignified and comical.

▲ Roxie and Fife enjoy high vantage points—here, on the porch steps, looking down on their summer garden by Mt. Monadnock in New Hampshire. Yellow verbascums, daylilies, yarrow, gray stachys, and white snakeroot thrive in the mountain air.

STREAM VALLEY
terriers

Plato and Socrates are rough-coated, companionable,
sturdy, prick-eared Norwich terriers who happen to be
brothers. Daily they walk the paths through their seven-
teen-acre garden in the gently rolling countryside of
western Delaware. They are usually joined by their master, landscape architect, author, and artist Bill Frederick,
who, over the last decade or two, planted this richly var-
ied stream valley with a painterly boldness.

The obvious place to start their daily adventure is the house, which is intriguingly built like a bridge across the running stream. From there, shadowy stone paths and steps pass a series of pools and woodland carpeted with wildflowers. More steps lead up and out to sunlight, lawns, and meadows planted with great, informal sweeps of perennials and massed strokes of a single shrub (thirty-five forsythia on a hillside, a vast bank of purple barberry, thirteen wisterias trained as trees). In early spring, the garden is still softly colored, lavender blues and greeny yellows with brushstrokes of gray and purple foliage. Later in May, the palette intensifies with startling swathes of red (banks of azaleas, blocks of tulips) played against purple and yellow. Twists and turns in the paths assure visual as well as olfactory surprises throughout the seasons in what Bill calls his "American stroll garden."

Five-year-olds Socrates and Plato adore those strolls with Bill and his wife Nancy, a wildflower enthusiast. Because of their rough tawny coats, these roly-poly terriers

▲ Norwich terrier brothers Plato and Socrates, on their daily walk past woodland and banks of spring bulbs in the Delaware garden that Bill Frederick created, like to pause with life-size figures of the Frederick children by sculptor Charles Cropper Park.

are sometimes hard to spot in the winter and early spring garden, camouflaged so well against a carpet of fallen leaves. Norwiches are hardy, weatherproof little dogs from England with happy-go-lucky attitudes. Short-legged, alert, and bright, they were valued as ratters originally, but now are treasured more for their delight-fully gregarious nature.

◀ Bill Frederick and Plato in a spring carpet of *Iris cristata.* A secluded kitchen terrace, perfect for sunning, is planted with squares of tulips and hyacinths. A frog (the work of New Mexico artist, Linda Lee Strong) no longer startles these strollers on a grass path between massed perennials and flowering dogwoods.

BEAGLES IN A
spring meadow

▲ Lula, Demon, and Reggie romp joyfully in their Pennsylvania garden—a daffodil-studded meadow, rimmed with dogwoods, just outside the house. The meadow slopes down to a pond—perfect for frog hunting.

When Kitty May created a garden just outside her charmingly quirky shingled house in rural Pennsylvania, she started with a meadow. She planted it with daffodils—thousands of them—for spring. She introduced Siberian iris to bloom in June, and the wonderful bushy, vibrant blue baptisia—both of which seeded and spread. In summer, she encouraged Queen Anne's lace to dust the meadow with white, and dug in jewel-like orange butterfly weed (*Asclepias*), which naturalized in the full sun. Asters, goldenrod, and boltonia were added to color the field in fall. Kitty ribboned the meadow with narrow mowed paths, set up a wire arbor and chairs in its midst for lingering with something to sip, then filled her flowering field with sniffing, hunting, baying beagles.

Lula was the cause of it all, Kitty says, the first beagle she and her husband Irenée owned, the one they fell in love with. Then came Demon, or Gioia, as she's called when

she's good, now five years old, a tri-color (black and white and brown), with a jaunty tail. Reginald is the latest addition, better known as Reggie, safely mature at the age of three.

Beagles are known for their cheerful, tranquil dispositions—even their "voice" is considered by devotees to be elegant and harmonious. They love nothing better than to wander in high grass, nosing about, flags (tails) up and waving. For them, a meadow is the perfect garden. For Kitty, it is a low-maintenance, natural, flower-studded delight.

◄ clockwise Nancy McCabe's Norfolk terrier mousing under a trough on her kitchen terrace; D'whinnie marks a thuja hedge in Quebec; miniature dachshund Noodle waits for the chance to chase Cleo the cat; Barbara Shattuck's Bernese mountain dogs, Theo and Winston, play tug-of-war; Norfolk puppy Roux after voles in the hosta.

up to no good

canine
GIANTS

A dog hip-high with a swooping tail and 150 pounds of muscular body residing in a small garden? Yes, indeed, and happily so, if he happens to be one of the large sight hounds—gentle, graceful beings who need no more than a twenty minute run to contentedly spend the rest of the day lying by your feet.

In a one-third-acre garden on the West Coast, landscape architect Katie Spitz and her husband, architect Dan Rhodes, live peacefully with an Irish wolfhound named Finnegan. The tallest of dogs, wolfhounds have a powerful, majestic presence that belies their sweet and sensitive nature. The only features possibly more

△ Sandy-colored Finnegan, the Irish wolfhound, reposing in his southern California garden among potted sedums and salvias.

dramatic than Finnegan in Katie's Santa Monica garden are two conical gazebos Dan built, and a double row of Italian cypress marching down her main grass path.

Because of his enormous size, six-year-old, sandy-coated Finnegan seems an astonishing garden companion to the uninitiated, an imposing presence among the potted herbs and phormiums or lying by Katie's chair on the dappled terrace. But wolfhounds and their close cousins, the deerhounds, are unusually nimble and quiet in their movements, rarely upsetting objects they pass or bounding recklessly about the yard.

In my garden at Duck Hill, in North Salem, New York,

Scottish deerhound May, a somewhat lesser giant with charcoal-gray coat, in my New York State garden.

May in the herb garden, and Finnegan lying on the terrace.

May was the second Scottish deerhound to keep me splendid company, along with one or two terriers. The formal part of the garden is about an acre in extent, but divided into small hedged-in rooms each with a different theme (the herb garden, the white garden, the hemlock garden) and crisscrossed with paths—seemingly a maze for an immensely tall, long-legged dog. When a pup, she loved to go on a gallop around the beds and in and out of the hedges as I stood there wincing, waiting to assess the damage. But there rarely was any. She certainly gave digging a whirl when she was young, seeing how much the

terriers (and I) seemed to enjoy it. She loved stealing my rubber kneeling pad and trotting around the garden with it before settling down for a chew.

As she grew older, in her aristocratic way she sensed, when loping along, that she should stick to the paths, and she rarely put a foot in a flower bed. Until cancer killed her at age seven, she was my most quiet and sweet companion outdoors, lying close by, front paws often elegantly crossed, as I weeded and pruned. I miss her great shaggy presence in the garden.

cairn
QUEBECOIS

The garden over which D'whinnie presides is an extraordinary accomplishment in the late twentieth century. It is as ambitious in plan as many of the grand eighteenth- and nineteenth-century estate gardens in France and England, but it is more personal, sparkling with humor and charm. Set on a hilltop above the St. Lawrence River in Quebec, this landscape of hedged allées and woodland walks, ponds, rills, fountains and reflecting pools, lupine meadows and delphinium borders, is the creation of garden visionary Frank Cabot.

Founder of the Garden Conservancy, Frank has spent his private time over the last twenty years enhancing the original bones of the garden he inherited that surrounds

his family's French-Canadian manor house. Deeply inter-
ested in the design of landscape, he extended his garden
vistas into the meadows and woodland that embrace the
property. He added architectural elements to surprise and
delight the eye—a moon bridge painted blue swooping
across one end of a pond, a forty-foot-tall arch framing a
view of the Laurentian Mountains, an exquisite Japanese
pavilion hidden in a wooded ravine, an elegant brick
pigeonnier at the end of an avenue of lindens. The garden
invites adventures. You have to answer a riddle to get the
door to open into the pigeon tower (where you can have
tea, or a party, or spend the night in a bedroom aerie). To
cross the ravine, you traverse swinging rope bridges that
can turn your knees into jelly. As you pass down one path

◀ D'whinnie views the
Canadian garden of Frank
Cabot from the porch, where
pots of fuchsias and agapanthus stand in summer.
Looking for bees in the lush
double borders of the perennial allée. A fine perspective
from the living room settee.

between hedges, you are suddenly serenaded by a life-size frog band made of bronze.

Frank and his wife, Anne, spend half their year traveling, the other half working in their Canadian garden, in the company of friends, as well as Scottish Highland cattle, ducks, geese, swans, two black cats, and, of course, D'whinnie.

D'whinnie, named after the single malt scotch Dalwhinnie (almost all the Cabot dogs have been named after whiskeys), is a cairn terrier more the color of champagne. Four years old, sturdy, feisty, with no doubt in his mind that he is boss, he rules his magnificent domain with a natural air. He watches the cows from the terrace steps, hunts frogs in the pond, teases the cat, and keeps Frank company as he divides and replants tiny alpines. Anne says D'whinnie is full of fun and vigor but not very obedient. "He doesn't come when you call if he's busy . . . which is most of the time."

Cairns, the smallest of the Scottish terriers, were valued as courageous working dogs, hunting vermin (rodents, weasels, foxes) in the rocks and ledges of their native land. They get their name from the rock piles, or cairns, scattered around the Highlands, that were the burial grounds of ancient Romans, and a haven for small destructive animals. Not as short-legged as the Norwich or Norfolk terrier, these mischievous sprites are more popular now as pets for the city or the country. They have a double coat, which can be any color but white, the inner fur soft and cottony, the outer coat rough and weather-proof.

▲ D'whinnie on the terrace where Frank Cabot plants his treasured alpines.

sitting pretty

▶ **clockwise** Noodle sunning on the terrace at Duck Hill; Carol Goldberg's Norfolk terriers, Rupert and Rachel, in their summer garden of blue anise hyssop, red beebalm and white shasta daisies; Bu, Jean Quaintance's Rottweiler, amidst agapanthus in San Francisco in February; golden retriever Miguel ornaments Bayberry Nursery on Long Island.

OLMSTED
garden mastiff

Set high above the ocean on the North Shore of Boston, a dazzling, sun-drenched garden of terraces and pools stretches out from a porch-wrapped Edwardian summer house, now used year-round. Gravel paths lead under white-painted arbors and pergolas draped with rambling roses and delicate clematis. Geometric panels of lawn divide beds of perennials, annuals, bulbs, and grasses, all flourishing in the sea air.

This is the home of Maggie (or Margaret Thatcher, as she is formally known). She is an English mastiff, 150 pounds of pure muscle, a watchdog of impressive proportions. Maggie does protect her five-year-old mistress,

Marguerite, accompanying her to the beach below the garden or keeping an eye on her from the balustrade beyond the front porch. But, like most mastiffs, she is sweet-natured, gentle, and quiet. "A couch potato," her owners, Nola Anderson and Jim Mullen, call her, for she spends much of her day lying on those velvet grass lawns.

The original bones of the garden—the stone walls and steps, the arbors and pools—were created by Frederic Law Olmsted, Jr. in 1906. But only vestiges of the formal design remained when Nola and Jim bought the property ten years ago. They rebuilt the walls, repaired the structures and pools, and, with the help of landscape architect

◀ Maggie the mastiff in front of a rambler-twined pergola. The garden that Maggie guards on the North Shore of Boston was designed in a series of terraces by Frederic Law Olmsted, Jr.

▲ Pots of agapanthus, as well as Maggie, decorate the waterlily pools. Lavender lines the walk above the tea garden where Maggie stands. A path runs from the house past softly-colored perennials to the water garden.

Patrick Chassé, filled the borders with an updated, vibrant display of flowers and foliage.

Maggie is one of three mastiffs who have overseen this garden restoration. Winston (Churchill) came first, a fawn-colored giant who was the supreme garden companion and loyal protector. He quietly shadowed Nola as she moved from border to border, lay by her side as she weeded, stood between her and any stranger who came to visit until she said it was okay. Sadly, he died of cancer at age four. Gus replaced Winston, but had a more restless nature. He started roaming on the beach; eventually, he was passed on to friends who had a cow farm. Maggie, however, continues Winston's tradition.

Mastiffs are an ancient breed. Caesar writes of how they fought beside their masters to defend Britain against

the Roman legions. These valiant English dogs were later brought to Rome for combat in the arena. Today, watching eight-year-old Maggie stroll past iris beds, water lily pools, and mixed flower borders, accompanying her diminutive mistress, I have trouble imagining the mastiff as the fierce fighting dog in the gladiators' pit.

empire of the
PEKINGESE

Blitz, Hercules, and Pandora on the steps to the crimson borders in their Cape Cod garden. Their mistress, Sarah Dunbar, favors the deep rich colors of plum, maroon, and red seen here, with stretches of gray-leaved plants for contrast.

Before I met Sarah and Scotty Dunbar's beloved mops, I had never seen a Pekingese close up, except in pictures. These treasured pets of the Chinese emperors, called lion dogs, are unlike any other breed, appearing to have no legs, no tail, almost no nose (at least not one that points), and ears neatly camouflaged by a heavy, flowing mane of hair. Of course, they do have legs, short and bowed (legend has it, so they would not wander from their imperial mistresses), and their tails are hidden under a fountain of silken hair.

"They're funny dogs," Sarah assures me, not only in looks but in personality. "They're very self-possessed, more like cats than dogs. They love you desperately, but

they have minds of their own." No matter how decora-
tive they look, they are not lap dogs, she insists. These
tough, independent-minded little creatures, according to
Sarah, like best to be outdoors.

Black-coated Blitz, ten years old (the alpha dog); six-
year-old, redhead Pandora; and young Hercules (at four, a
giant peke at eighteen pounds) spend their happiest hours
with the Dunbars nosing around in their four-acre garden
on Cape Cod. Sarah and Scotty are keen gardeners who
pack up their station wagon with dogs and plants every

spring and drive up to Massachusetts from their home-town of New Orleans to spend as much time as possible working in their garden. Lingering often until November, they plant flower borders and trees, and plot new design schemes. Dreams of grottos, obelisks, ruins, and water gardens fill their heads.

Wide borders of shrubs and perennials in shades of yellow, cream, and chartreuse greet you as you approach the charming old seaside house. A stone-walled garden room, green walks, specimen trees, and a potager prom-ise horticultural richness. The perspective from the terrace leads down double herbaceous borders lushly planted with

▲ The three pekes flop on the lawn in front of a boldly-planted shade border.

crimson flowers and gray and plum foliage. These are the result of a collaboration with English designer Tim Rees, as is the rest of the garden. "We tweak it together," Sarah says, when Tim periodically crosses the Atlantic. But she and Scotty do most of the work.

Sarah loves the richness of deep colors, the ruby red of dahlias, the black of hollyhocks, the dark purple of *Buddleia* 'Black Knight'. Pandora, Blitz, and Hercules add their own red and raven shades to the garden, when they deign to linger there. They do have wanderlust, Sarah says, despite their short legs, and will disappear "the minute your back is turned" into the hedgerow to spy on the neighbors.

▲ The garden by the Dunbar's seaside house is terraced with stone walls and steps. From vibrantly-colored double flower borders, you walk down to an area of calm with ever-green plantings and lawn.

the luxury

of lawns

◀ clockwise Miguel and Beasly
are half-hidden in the longer grass
of their backyard flowering meadow
in Long Island; Dido lazily luxuriates in
front of ancient yews; Winston, six-
month-old Bernese mountain dog,
cools down between capers; Fanny
massages her back; Elizabeth, the
whippet, wants to play, but Lucy would
rather roll in the grass.

Chloe, a two-year-old Jack Russell terrier, poses (for a second) before one of the famed daylily borders in this Connecticut garden. Then she's back to playing ball.

Sydney Eddison is famed for her color-rich daylily borders and books on gardening. She has a flair for mingling the vibrant hues of her daylilies, which she has by the hundreds, with summer perennials, grasses, and shrubs, to make stunning pictures. In late spring, her primrose-littered woodland is an enchanting place. For fourteen years, Sydney shared her Newtown, Connecticut garden with a sweet, gentle Jack Russell terrier bitch named Abby. Abby died two years ago, and Sydney immediately sought to fill the aching void with a like-minded puppy. Into her life came the dog from hell.

Chloe is a young, gorgeous, smooth coat, tri-color Jack Russell with an inclination to bite. Upon entering her new home as a fetching tyke, she set about routinely nipping Sydney's husband, Martin—as well as just about anybody else, save her mistress. Being a soft-hearted animal lover,

Sydney did not cart Chloe off to the animal shelter so she could get back to gardening peacefully. She knew giving up on Chloe meant sure death for the dog. No one else would cope with such pint-size aggression. So she hired a personal trainer and a dog psychiatrist and worked daily, weekly, to convince Chloe that life in a garden—for dogs as well as people—soothes anger, quells distrust, positively consumes wired-up energy.

Chloe is close to being cured of her habit. She helps Sydney with the garden chores, climbs into the apple trees for a better view of things, plays ball with the agility of a soccer star. However, she is now struggling for her life. Undiagnosed Lyme disease, the scourge of gardeners on the East Coast, resulted in kidney failure. Sydney feels certain that Chloe will revive. "She's so tough and ornery, I think she'll make it."

POODLES BY
the pool

David Rubin and his wife Susan moved recently to an old brick rectory fifty miles north of Manhattan. They brought with them their daughter, Josephine Violet, their two standard poodles, Scarlet and Aretha, and a greenhouse-worth of tropical plants.

David had in mind borders of hot-colored, bold-foliaged, tender plants around the rectangular pool below the terrace just like ones he had nurtured and enjoyed at his old property. Seven years ago, he caught the gardening bug quite by accident when he asked garden designer Hitch Lyman to help him landscape around a turquoise, kidney-shaped pool, and Hitch suggested a Caribbean fan-

tasy. Together they planted banana trees, cannas, hedychiums, castor beans, and coleus, ordered from mail-order catalogs. David rented a greenhouse, and learned to grow his tender tropicals from cuttings and seeds.

When David moved to his new home, he decided on a patterned vegetable and flower garden near the house. Primroses and native flora would be planted by the stream at the edge of the property. But around the pool, he wanted to repeat his flashy, big-leaved, tropical borders. Between the bluestone edging and the protective wooden fence, he dug narrow beds and skillfully planted golden-striped cannas, burgundy-leaved castor beans, beet-red

◀ All-white Scarlet in the tropical jungle David Rubin grows around his Bedford, New York pool. Aretha keeps young Josephine company by the vegetable garden.

amaranths dripping pipe-cleaner flowers, banana trees, elephant ears, and hibiscus with crimson blooms like saucers. The plants grow to prodigious size in the heat of summer, creating a jungle enclosure. That Aretha and Scarlet, the Rubins' statuesque poodles, happen to be ink-black and chalk-white, contrasting gorgeously with the wildly-colored flowers and foliage, is no doubt an accidental bonus.

Standard poodles, with their proud air and intense, piercing eyes, give the unsettling impression of being more perceptive and intelligent than you are. They are known to love human company and abhor solitude. Eight-year-old Aretha, David says, has not acknowledged that she's really a dog. He describes her as protective and needy, wanting constant attention. For example, "just as you're drifting off to sleep in a comfortable chair," he says, "she'll come over with a toy." Scarlet, two years younger, is easy-going, docile, and very playful. The two poodles, along with

▲ Aretha with hibiscus and elephant ears. The two standard poodles pose in front of white cosmos.

daughter Josephine, are David's companions in the garden.
They have learned by now not to step in his flower beds.

Originally bred as gun dogs in Europe (the French call
them *caniche*, or duck dogs), poodles were skilled at
retrieving ducks from muddy lakes. In order to make
swimming easier, the coat on their hindquarters was shorn,
but puffs of dense hair were left to protect their joints
from rheumatism. Scarlet and Aretha, elegantly clipped and
coifed, however, are firmly discouraged from trying their
sport in the tropical pool.

dog haven, CONNECTICUT

Bunny Williams escapes the city and her demanding work as one of America's top decorators by hopping into a car every weekend and driving to her nineteenth-century farm in northwestern Connecticut. Accompanying her are her dogs—Brewster, a fifteen-year-old Norfolk terrier, five-year-old Charlie (an irresistible mixture of airedale and terrier), and three-year-old Lucy, a sweet, salt-and-pepper mutt rescued from the streets of Atlanta. Also in the car is four-year-old Elizabeth, the whippet Bunny shares (along with the Connecticut house) with her partner, antique dealer John Rosselli.

For the dogs, as well as for Bunny, the farm is a blissful retreat—plump sofas and beds for napping and pastoral

▲ Charlie, the mutt, and Elizabeth, the whippet, at the boxwood-bordered fish pool in the center of Bunny Williams's flower garden.

acres to explore. There are butterflies flitting in the flower borders, chickens and doves to tease as they strut around the aviary, a reflecting pool and ponds for fishing, rows of vegetables to romp through, and stretches of lawn to roll on.

For twenty-two years, Bunny has been fine-tuning her country place inside and out, adding gardens and garden rooms. A screen porch and vine-draped loggia now look out to yew topiaries and a box-hedged pool flanked by mixed flower borders. From a plant-filled conservatory off the guesthouse (formerly the barn and garage), you have a view of the potager—Bunny's favorite spot, patterned with herbs and flowers. A large working garden for vegetables and cutting flowers is a recent addition, together with a greenhouse

Charlie, part airedale, part terrier, strides past lawn chairs. Lucy, also a mutt, looks for action in the walled garden beyond Bunny's country loggia and kitchen bay.

for forcing bulbs and growing auriculas and camelias.

As an interior designer, Bunny instinctively knows how important permanent structure is in a garden. She uses arbors, pergolas, trellises, and low hedges as frames, large stone vases, clay pots, and round boxwood bushes as accents. They add immeasurably to the charm of the place. Four rollicking dogs serendipitously add a fillip to the scene.

Brewster, the Norfolk, was a fancy show dog until he was two, when his breeder retired him because of an overbite. Bunny adopted him, buck teeth and all, and he became her loyal shadow. Once, on a lark, she entered him in a local dog show, certain he'd win the day. Brewster walked in the ring and promptly lay down. He'd

▲ Mostly-terrier mutt Lucy and Elizabeth cavort on the lawn in front of the fenced-in kitchen garden, Bunny's favorite spot on her property.

been there, done that, now he liked being a lap dog. Elizabeth, Charlie, and Lucy are more spirited, cavorting, playing tug-of-war, chasing each other around the garden. Bunny says Elizabeth is a typical whippet, sweet but independent, mischievous, and full of beans.

Ever since bringing Charlie home from the Humane Society (he jumped in her lap and she was smitten) and rescuing the homeless Lucy, Bunny has sung the praises of adopting mixed breeds. She and her friend Kitty Hawks recently started a foundation called "Tails in Need" in order to raise money for abandoned dogs. The first event, The Great American Mutt Show (categories, Mostly Labrador Class, Mostly Shepherd Class, Best Lap Dog Over Fifty Pounds, etc.), is a benefit for the Humane Society of New York. Bunny says Lucy is the perfect advertisement for shelter adoption. "She's a star dog— always happy, friendly (she would jump into anyone's lap), adorable looking. She has charisma."

▲ Brewster, Bunny's old Norfolk terrier, checks out the hyacinth bulbs in the greenhouse. Dog hellos.

hot dogs

◀ clockwise Beasly, Sponk, and Miguel—all rescued by garden-book publisher Ngaere Macray and landscape architect David Seeler—swim at their summer garden; Bluebell, a blue merle Shetland sheepdog, and Poppy, a red merle Australian shepherd, on an Indian summer day in Pepe Maynard's Bedford, New York garden; Springer cools off in his waterfront garden on Long Island Sound; Mango, a young King Charles spaniel, gets her ears wet in Tim Rees's London garden; Fanny emerges from a dip.

barnsley at MADOO

When you go to visit Madoo, the wonderfully quirky garden of American painter Robert Dash (it is open to the public two days a week), you might not catch a glimpse of Barnsley. He is probably in his very own flowery yard, fenced with pickets and an arched gate topped with red balls, and containing a doghouse just right in size for a chunky Norfolk terrier. In summer, Barnsley's place is overrun with tiny ruby-colored morning glories, chartreuse nicotiana, and purple *Verbena bonariensis*.

The two-acre garden in Sagaponack, Long Island is yet another painted canvas for Bob Dash, perhaps his *chef d'oeuvre*, a bold play of colors and shapes in a series of intimate outdoor rooms, each with a different mood, an

▲ Norfolk terrier Barnsley finds some interesting tree stumps at Madoo on Long Island.

unexpected twist. Wooden architecture abounds in the garden—gates, bridges, arbors, fences, posts, benches—often painted vivid colors. The brilliant strokes of yellow, purple, chartreuse, royal blue, and red are a theme, a hallmark of Bob's garden. Even the doors of the two brown-shingled cottages (one for winter use, the other for summer) are eye-stoppers in his garden pictures because of their startlingly fresh colors.

Paths, varying from sawed rounds of telephone poles to large pebbles washed smooth and round, meander through the garden, from surprise to surprise. In his beguiling book, *Notes from Madoo*, Bob speaks of his love of Indian paths, "rather like the secret walks small children

Barnsley trots across the water garden on Robert Dash's whimsical oriental bridge.

make," and this is what you're reminded of as you wend your way from hedged-in borders exploding with flowers and vegetables, to ginkgo grove to water garden to rose allée. If you're lucky, you'll be accompanied on the adventure by Bob and Barnsley.

Barnsley is named after Rosemary Verey's very famous garden in Oxfordshire, and she is also his godmother. When the doyenne of English gardens calls from across the Atlantic to chat with her old friend, Bob invariably asks

▲ Ruby morning glories, mulleins, and verbena flourish in Barnsley's own enclosed garden.

if she'd like to talk to her god-dog. The phone is turned over to Barnsley, who snuffles appropriately.

Like all Norfolk terriers, Barnsley is rough-coated and robust, a jaunty, low-to-the-ground, stocky little beast. He is typically inquisitive and happy-go-lucky. His ears drop close to his cheeks, which is the only way he differs from his cousin, the Norwich. Both breeds are considered among the smallest of the working terriers. As I have a Norfolk of my own, I know he is a dandy companion in the country garden.

▲ Barnsley strolls past boxwood balls underplanted with golden lysimachia in the ginkgo grove.

fanny in the FLOWERS

Ice Pond Farm, the home of Olympic skater Dick Button
and his airedale Fanny, is surrounded by maple-lined fields
and a white-pine and beech woodland. It overlooks a
dammed stream that widens briefly into a mirrored pool
of water, where, a century ago, ice was gathered. As you
approach the garden past old bumpy-trunked apple trees,
Fanny would burst out of the farmhouse and come

bounding toward you, ears and tail up, in enthusiastic greeting. But this past winter, with the garden put to bed, she died, quietly, of grand old age.

The black-and-tan airedale terrier, lively, good-natured, and straightforward, seemed just right as a companion for Dick, and a perfect complement to the garden they shared. It is an exuberant garden, full of light-hearted color

▲ Airedale Fanny and Dick Button in their country garden, north of New York City, full of brilliant summer flowers.

and pizzazz in summer, and yet it is down-to-earth, blowsy, with a mixture of vegetables, bright annuals, and perennials. Sunflowers nod above wild-looking species marigolds and red-ribbed Swiss chard; zinnias mingle with flowering dill, leeks, and chives; poke weed, castor bean, and cardoons shoot up through lavender blue asters and brassy yellow heleniums. Lab-lab beans and morning glories twine around twig teepees and tall scarlet tithonias play against the duller mauvy-red heads of our native Joe-Pye weed.

Fanny always joined her master and his guests for walks through the flowers, trotting ahead, then looking back protectively. Sometimes, she would wander off on the grass paths that lead into fields studded with fruit trees and berry

▲ Fanny rounds the bend below a sculpture that is the stone rim of an old well standing on end. Dick calls it 'Watch out for the Hole in the Ice.' Fanny strolls through the garden past asters and nicotiana.

bushes, or down to the swimming pool with a view to the ice pond below. Here, surrounded by more billowing flowers—cranesbills, geraniums, nicotiana, catmint, and thymes, she would have a quick dip.

Although the airedale is called a terrier, the breed has some hound blood in its ancestry and is much larger and longer legged than the usual "go-to-ground" creatures we think of as terriers, who so easily scoot down holes and tunnels after rodents and rabbits. Still, he is a capable hunter, able to track deer and bear as well as badgers and otter. He has the hound's sweet disposition but the terrier's agility, and, more important, his buoyant spirit. Fanny's spirit certainly lives on at Ice Pond Farm.

provençal
PUP

Toby, a six-month-old wheaten terrier with mischief on his mind, gleefully disrupts "the equilibrium" so brilliantly achieved in this Luberon garden by designer Nicole de Vesian. Typical of her style, it is a garden not about color but about the harmony of textures and shapes arranged in patterns and played against each other using the plants of Provence. The venerable Madame de Vesian, who died recently, might have rolled her eyes at Toby cavorting in her tightly-clipped and elegantly-controlled landscape of herbs and trees. But I think not. Even the most studied, balanced, and restricted garden needs an element of surprise, a hair out of place, to give it a sense of charm.

Toby's owners, New Yorkers who treasure their French garden of stone-walled terraces, cypresses, and topiary balls of fragrant rosemary, teucrium, lavender, and box, prefer their landscape to be hopping with children

and friends. A rambunctious puppy is a happy addition.

Before he entered her life, Toby's mistress researched what sort of dog they might get. But, her husband and twin boys spied Toby in a pet shop window on a New York City street, went in, got licked, and fell in love. A deposit was put down for the dog. "Absolutely no," said the boys' mother, "we're not getting some dog from a pet store. Get the deposit back." Her husband refused. So she went herself to retrieve the deposit . . . and, in turn, fell in love with the dog.

Toby has a beautiful, soft, honey-colored coat—the wheaten of his name, appearing as a dash of welcome color in the garden of grays and greens. He seems to be smiling much of the time. He is somewhat larger than most terriers, but upholds their most typical characteristic—an inextinguishable *joie de vivre*.

▲ Toby, the young, mischievous wheaten terrier enjoying his summer garden of clipped herbs in Provence.

◄ clockwise Professional gardener Steve Bell travels by bicycle in Austin, Texas, with his fifteen-year-old dog, Indra; sign on a New Hampshire roadside; Talya, a venerable vizsla in a July garden in New Hampshire; Annabelle, Melissa Orme's golden retriever, in her Connecticut garden; Jake, Jennifer Myers's hound dog in Texas; Maltese Scruffy with hydrangeas in Easthampton.

old dogs in the garden

DOGS TO THE
manor born

Carved in stone below one of the balustrades at Englefield House in Berkshire, England, is the following quotation from its seventeenth-century owner: "If you help towards Englefield garden either in flowers or invention you shall be welcome thither." In fact, Sir William and Lady Benyon are not so exacting—they welcome all who come to enjoy the seven-acre garden that surrounds their honey-colored, turreted, Elizabethan house.

The lace-trimmed manor house sits on a terraced plateau, rather like a confection on a platter, with a view below of a vast deer park—a typically eighteenth-century English landscape of ancient trees clustered on gently rolling ground, a lake, browsing deer. Formal terraces of lawn extend out from the house and are framed by richly planted flower borders, backed by stone walls and

balustrades. Up a series of staircases, the garden relaxes into open woodland, with specimen trees and carpets of wildflowers and bulbs.

This is the domain of Elizabeth Benyon, a devoted gardener. Although the renowned American-born designer, Lanning Roper, helped update the formal garden in the 1970s, replacing parterres of roses with herbaceous borders and panels of lawn, Lady Benyon orchestrates the plantings and color schemes herself. She is accompanied in all her garden activities by Plum, her Jack Russell terrier, and Finny, the young black labrador retriever (that is, when he is not off duck hunting with Sir William). Of course,

▲ The extensive gardens and park that surround Englefield House in Berkshire, England, are a grand playground for the Labrador retriever, Finny, and Plum, the Jack Russell terrier.

Plum has her own agenda, hunting for rabbits in the stone
walls; Finny is naturally content to lie down on the lawns
or cool stone steps while his mistress works.

The Benyons' is a garden on a grand scale, and yet, like
the manor house itself, it has an appearance of lighthearted-
edness. Perhaps it has to do with the whimsical surprises
scattered about the property—an ivy-covered gazebo with
a ferny seat hidden in the shrubbery; a life-size bear, carved
from a felled oak tree, standing on his hind legs by the
woodland walk; a children's garden with an entrance just

big enough for a six-year-old, miniature hedges, little seats, and secret water jets. It also has to do with the presence of Plum and Finny, the one scampering about, the other quietly wagging his tail, as you stroll about the garden.

Jack Russell terriers have become immensely popular as country pets in England and America, although they were recognized by the American Kennel Club only recently. Developed as a breed by an English clergyman in the 1800s, and named after him, they are similar in looks to fox terriers, but smaller. Whether long-legged or short, smooth-coated or rough, Jack Russells are loved by their owners for their merriment and daring. Labrador retrievers, of course, are not only superior duck hunters and seeing-eye dogs, but everyone's idea of a family dog, ever amiable and affectionate.

◀ Plum on the balustrade above the herbaceous borders. Plum and Finny in front of the Benyon's Elizabethan house.

ASSISTANT gardener

Robin Zitter is a young, professional gardener with an extensive knowledge of plants and a flair for creating flower borders of fresh charm. Vivid coloring, a cottagey looseness in planting, and imaginative combinations of annuals, bulbs, and perennials, are her trademarks. She divides her weeks among a few private gardens in Connecticut and New York, as well as the public garden at the Bellany Ferriday House in Bethlehem, which she tends with an artist's eye. Her constant companion in these gardens is Luna, a sweet-looking, slightly-built dog, part border collie, part shepherd, that she rescued five years ago from the pound. Luna sits in the passenger seat of the white truck Robin drives, her head out the window as they speed from home to the designated garden of the day. While

▲ Luna keeps watch while her mistress works in Netta Lockwood's garden north of New York City. The path to the greenhouse is made with round slices of tree trunks set in gravel.

Robin works, Luna lies patiently nearby, barking in warning
if anyone new approaches. She is a one-woman dog,
intensely devoted to her hard-working mistress.

Robin's favorite days are spent with Luna caring for
Netta Lockwood's enchanting garden just an hour north
of Manhattan. Here she oversees a richly diverse landscape of oak woodland, rock ravines, meadow, pond, and
orchard—clearing paths, pruning the many specimen
flowering trees, planting new young shrubs and trees. She
grows her flowers from seed and cuttings in the greenhouse that is billowing with scented geraniums, or in the
deep cold frames by the vegetable garden. If you walk
from the house along the mowed grass path through the
apple trees in the orchard, you come upon Netta's secret

garden of circular and triangular flower beds, inspired by an old knot garden pattern. Around Netta's original plantings of tree peonies, roses, and clematis, Robin now plants her colorful annuals, bulbs, and perennials.

Twenty years ago, when Netta was in her seventies, she hired Robin straight out of New York Botanical Garden's professional horticultural program to come help her in her garden. A woman of graciousness and compassion, with an extraordinary sense of style, and a love of flowers and trees, Netta was an ideal mentor for Robin. Over time, they became best friends, working together in the garden, learning, experimenting, loving it equally.

▲ In the knot garden, Luna is surrounded by lady's mantle, germander, purple salvias, lavender blue ageratum, and variegated-leaved scarlet and gold nasturtiums.

Luna shared their intimacy for the last five years. And because she and Robin spent so much more time in Netta's garden than in their own, she came to treat it as her place, guarding the path to the greenhouse or lying among the nasturtiums and lavender blue ageratum.

artful dogs

◀ clockwise Barnsley oblivious to Matisse at Madoo; Plum and Finny feeling bearish at Englefield House; Chotsie and Allan Blank's King Charles spaniel, Winston, with hydrangeas and plump diver in their Cape Cod garden; Beasly, Miguel, and Sponk hang out with coyote friends behind David Seeler's Bayberry Nursery on Long Island; dachsund Toby in Sir Reresby and Lady Sitwell's London town garden.

french frou-frou
IN THE HEART
of texas

Minou and Chouette, soignée, silken, three-year-old
Maltese sisters who were born in France, live in a garden
as glamorous as they are—deep in the heart of Texas. It is
primarily a green garden, surrounding a 1920s white lime-
stone house that opens to cooling, old-world loggias, a
garden all about shade and water. Situated between two
busy streets in Austin, the property is dominated by magnificent live oaks and cedar elms, which afford shade as
well as privacy. With the help of English garden designer
Penelope Hobhouse, and French designer Jean Louis
Raynaud, the present owners added a variety of water

74

features—pools, rills, fountains, a lake—that soothe the soul as well as the body in the heat of a Texan summer.

A tour of the property, with sprightly Minou and Chouette underfoot or tucked under their mistress's arm, might start at the pool garden designed by Penny Hobhouse off one side of the house. A narrow canal, or rill, is set in brick terracing and bounded by flower borders that are Persian in feeling, with a scented vine-laden pergola at the far end. Across the lawn on the other side of the house, more dramatic stone terracing is cut with water rills. The water source starts at a pool and fountain against the house wall and spills down several levels into a limestone-bordered, swiftly-running creek. These bold terraces were thought up by Jean Louis Raynaud not only

▲ Little Maltese Minou and Chouette, born in France, live in a Texas garden. Fountains, rills, and canals course through the garden and end in a lake full of water lilies.

⏴ The belvedere, appearing magically at the end of the lake, was inspired by one at Versailles. The two Maltese, as well as their owners, find the sound of water cooling in the heat of a Texas summer.

for entertaining, but to link the theme of water from the house to the lake at the end of the property.

If you follow the shaded stone path as it descends along the ferny creek, pausing while the two Maltese dab at a floating leaf, you will suddenly catch a first glimpse of the lake studded with water lilies; a few more steps and the whole romantic picture is revealed—a Monet-like pond rimmed with iris and, at its far edge, a French folly: the belvedere, inspired by a similar one in the gardens at the Petit Trianon at Versailles. What could be more appropriate as a setting for two lively Gallic sprites?

Chouette and Minou come from an ancient breed, considered more spaniel than terrier, affectionate, lively, upper-crust dogs from the Mediterranean with a hardiness that belies their size. Titian painted their portraits, as did Goya and Sir Joshua Reynolds. According to the first Queen Elizabeth's doctor, these highbred dogs were "sought after for the pleasure and amusement of women" who carried them "in their bosoms, in their beds, and in their arms while in their carriages." Certainly Minou and Chouette are more of this century, with their feet firmly on the ground.

fauna behind the
GARDEN GATE

The purpose of the high white board fence and gate
Michael Brennan built, which encloses the entrance to his
Victorian house in Syracuse, New York, and separates it
from the driveway and front walk, was to keep Fauna in.
But Fauna kept barking every time someone arrived for a
visit, frustrated she couldn't see who it was coming up the
drive. So Michael cut a small square window in the gate,
just big enough for Fauna to put her head through. A gin-
ger head and ears, grizzled white snout, dark eyes and
nose now appear when you walk up the flagstone path
from the driveway to the gate, which is itself framed
within a pagoda-like arch painted blue-green and white
and dripping with honeysuckle and clematis.

There were other reasons for the fence. It would

block the view of parked cars from the house, and, more importantly, create a south-facing wall. Michael is a professional landscape gardener and lover of plants who knows, like every gardener in a cold climate, how wonderful it is to have a south wall. Here in the baking sun, he grows euphorbias, and yuccas, and all the herbs that like it hot and dry, letting flowers seed in the gravel.

Michael and his partner, theater director Robert Moss, adopted Fauna from the Humane Society not as a pup but as an older dog. They have found it a perfect arrangement. Fauna, now eight, is loyal, calm, undyingly grateful, and past puppy mischief. Allegedly part corgi, part German shepherd, she is Michael's sidekick in the garden, while he is weeding, planting, and walking the mowed paths through the fields. And although she loves her window in the garden gate, she still likes barking her greeting.

Michael Brennan built a window in his garden gate, so Fauna could look outside to see who's coming. While Michael tends his Syracuse garden, Fauna is his loyal sidekick.

dido at doddington place

Doddington Place, the home of Richard Oldfield and his wife Amicia de Moubray in Kent—not far from Sissinghurst and Leeds Castle—is a Victorian family house surrounded by ten acres of extraordinary gardens. They are open to the public every Wednesday in spring and summer, which Richard says is an excellent discipline. ("If we didn't have members of the public wandering around, rightly critical . . . we would certainly be a great deal sloppier.") The garden is also the site (with the grand yews as backdrop) of an annual opera performance.

Vistas, specimen trees, and venerable yew hedges are the most memorable features of the place. The garden is embraced by orchards, park, and farmland offering pastoral views beyond the hedges and allées of trees. But there is also a woodland garden, unique in this chalky part of the world for having a pocket of acid moist soil where rhododendrons, camellias, and azaleas flourish. There is a walk of wellingtonias, planted in the 1850s, a spring garden, a pond walk with an avenue of European mountain ash, an Edwardian rock garden, and a sunken garden near the house with mixed flower borders tended by Amicia, who is an avid gardener. Plaques set in the terrace wall

▲ Dido, the brown-spotted dalmation, in front of the ancient yews where summer operas are performed at Doddington Place in Kent, England. White Japanese anemones bloom in the rock garden in September.

above the sunken garden commemorate several generations of Oldfield dogs buried there. And then, there is Dido.

Four-year-old Dido is a happy, somewhat rotund and placid dalmatian—startlingly white, of course, but with brown spots not black. Her liver coloring is quite unusual and distinctive. The Oldfields smilingly call her "the greedy dalmatian," because she has an uncontrollable fondness for food. (An English nickname for the breed is the Plum Pudding Dog.) The dalmatian—agile, intelligent, and striking in appearance—has been valued in war, as a shepherd, a ratter, a sporting dog, a firehouse mascot, a circus performer, and, above all, a coaching dog. Dido, however, spends her days at Doddington, not trotting alongside carriages, but rolling in the velvet grass in front of the cloud-like yews, nosing around the rock garden, or licking the face (probably sweetly sticky) of three-year-old Edward, the Oldfields' son.

The basic design of Dido's marvelous garden, including the planting of the great trees and those impressive yews,

▲ Dido yawns in front of an avenue of European mountain ash. In the late afternoon sunlight, Dido gets some loving from his diminutive master, Edward Oldfield.

occurred in 1910 under the direction of Richard's uncle's aunt. One section of hedge near the house was allowed to grow untended during the Second World War, and has since been clipped in natural contours. (Amicia writes that visitors have described the hedge as looking like a series of gorillas seen from the rear.) Two tons of yew clippings result from Richard and his helper's hedge trimming, which happens once a year in late summer. The clippings are sold to a pharmaceutical firm to be processed into Taxol, a drug used to fight cancer.

snow dogs

▲ clockwise Casper in Renny Reynolds and Jack Staub's Pennsylvania garden; long-haired German shepherds Garbo and Gunther on Jackie and Peter Kamenstein's millhouse terrace with its dramatic waterfall; Schuyler, the golden retriever, and Gracie, the corgi, are ready to come in from the winter garden; Noodle on the move.

merry duo
IN ILLINOIS

Forest waits for company in the conservatory at Craig Bergmann and James Grigsby's home near Chicago. Tibetan terriers Rosie and Forest nestle among grasses and hydrangeas in the autumn garden at Craig and James's nursery.

Rosie and Forest are Tibetan terriers who live in Illinois, not Tibet, and, in fact, are not terriers at all. Mistakenly named when the breed was first brought to England in the 1930s, these delightful Tibetan creatures do not dig burrows into the earth (*la terre* of terrier) in search of varmints. They were never considered working dogs, but from the beginning were treasured as companions, almost as part of the family. Playful and affectionate, they are medium small dogs, resembling miniature versions of old English sheepdogs, with a thick long double coat and snowshoe feet to weather the harsh climate of their native land. They have exceptional agility and surefootedness, the better to handle the mountain terrain of Tibet, or, more to the point, to leap effortlessly onto a bed to wake its occupant with kisses. At least that's how a guest staying with

Craig Bergmann and James Grigsby is greeted by these merry dogs first thing in the morning.

Craig and James are prominent garden designers in the Chicago area. They live in Wilmette in a small house surrounded by a tiny garden where every inch of space is decorated with tapestries of plants—in pots or in the

ground. Fuchsias, coleus, and geraniums with patterned leaves spill from window boxes and tubs. Topiary boxwood, clipped myrtles, more scented geraniums, and asters in season, stand clustered in old clay pots by the entrance to the garden. Species roses and clematis climb the walls under beds of lilies, shrub roses, verbascums, campanulas, and salvias. Orchids and begonias hang from the beams of the old greenhouse attached to one end of their house—Craig and James's favorite spot for evening drinks with the dogs.

Rosie and Forest are their children—their dancing shadows at home, in the garden, at the nursery they run in Winter Harbor, on their rounds to clients' gardens, and on walks along Lake Michigan. Rosie, short for *Rhododendron* 'Roseum Elegans', was born on Valentine's day, and is becoming slightly less puppyish at age fourteen. Her long hair is black with strokes of white on her head, her snout, her chest, and her paws. Four-year-old Forest is black all over except for a blaze of white on his chest. When he leaps and twirls, his fine coat twirls too like a silken fringe.

▲ Rosie heads down the garden path past sedums in a ceramic log, and becomes self-conscious in front of a pot of fuchsias.

halloween
WATER DOGS

Nina Wood shares her French fantasy of a house with husband Peter, two grown daughters, two grandchildren, three Portuguese water dogs, one miniature poodle, and a mostly-bearded-collie mutt. It was a rather plain, ordinary house, Nina says, when they moved there in the 1960s, but it looked out onto an apple orchard and meadows, and was in easy driving distance of Manhattan.

Home from a few years of living in Paris, where Nina designed fanciful headdresses for Yves St. Laurent, she transformed her American house into a miniature chateau. She added a tower, just big enough for a bedroom, hung chalky, French blue shutters, and planted vines to climb up the stuccoed walls. On either side of the front door, in round stone vases, she planted a winged euonymus that she dug up in the woods (where this Asian shrub is invading the natural flora), and cleverly trained each into an elegantly graceful tree. She created a walled, graveled courtyard, similar to ones you would see in Europe, with an old carved column in the middle, surrounded by pots of boxwood. Here in summer she erects awnings of Indian

▲ Nina Wood's three Portuguese water dogs, miniature poodle, and bearded-collie mutt cluster at the front door and in the courtyard of her Gallic-inspired home in New York.

bedspreads, and the whole family shares leisurely meals with friends, the dogs sprawled at their feet. In autumn, pumpkins decorate the courtyard walls and a great arching catalpa drops its burnished yellow leaves on the gravel.

Dogs are everywhere, coddled, adored, allowed the run of the garden, and, indoors, the best of the silk upholstered Louis XV chairs and tapestry-draped sofas. Fortunately, the intelligent and spirited Portuguese water dogs, like poodles, have non-shedding coats. Robust and wooly-haired, they were used originally to herd fish into nets. Because of their hardiness, they are superb outdoor dogs. Chessie, Sam, and Baby, Nina's water dogs, have a grand time inside and out.

WESTIE in foliage

Serena Bass is known as a chic caterer in New York City and as the doyenne of Serena, a popular bar she owns in the Chelsea Hotel. What the cognoscenti probably don't know is that she makes marvelous gardens. On her property in North Salem, New York, she transformed a yard of wet reeds and swampy field behind her house into a brilliantly-colored collage of shrubs, perennials, bulbs, and grasses that grew to prodigious sizes in the damp sunshine. This is where Serena's West Highland terrier Ruby came as a puppy, growing up in the garden, scooting in and out the dog door to race on the lawn and disappear in the reeds.

Three-year-old Ruby is "brilliant, a Mensa candidate," according to Serena. "She's a mind reader. When I go to pick up my sneakers, she's at the door." Ruby fetches sticks from the local pond, having learned by watching a labrador when she was a pup. She didn't know she was an earth-burrowing dog, Serena says. "She's the soul of peacefulness until she sees there's something to do. Then she's a demon doer." Ruby is fastidious in her likes and dislikes, and is happy as long as she's with her mistress.

Serena lives in the city now—in the meat market district ("Do you know what joy that is for a dog?"), and Ruby's garden is on their rooftop. However, they come out to visit their old home frequently. Seldom is a garden

kept up after its creator moves away, but the new owners have maintained Serena's garden very much as it always was. Last October, Ruby and Serena found the garden a tawny beauty, the burnished red barberries and yellowed Siberian iris playing against the grays of stachys, pinks, and caryopteris in the garden beds. In sweeps around the lawn, burgundy and golden grasses mingled with shiny red twig dogwoods and buttery clethra, and the autumn trees themselves echoed the colors in the distance.

▲ Ruby in the autumn garden of ornamental grasses, barberries, buddleias, and perennials created by her mistress, Serena Bass, in North Salem, New York.

tail ends

▸ **clockwise** Kathie Weymouth's corgi pauses by the gate in her Fishers Island garden; Barnsley takes a break at Madoo; Maggie surveys the beach from the garden balustrade; four-month-old puppy Roux navigates the garden steps; Dido nosing along in the Edwardian rock garden.